BLUES HARMONICA

for beginners

Alfred, the leader in educational publishing,
and the National Guitar Workshop,
one of America's finest guitar schools, have joined
forces to bring you the best, most progressive
educational tools possible. We hope you will enjoy
this book and encourage you to look for
other fine products from Alfred and the
National Guitar Workshop.

An Easy Beginning Method

ROB FLETCHER

Acquisition, editorial: Nathaniel Gunod, Workshop Arts
Music typesetting, assistant editorial and photo acquisition: Joe Bouchard
Photography (harmonicas, Rob Fletcher): Stuart Rabinowitz
CD recorded at Bar None Studios, Cheshire, CT
Cover illustration: Rich Borge

Contents

About the Author 3

Introduction 4

Chapter 1—Beginning the Blues 5
Holding the Harmonica—
            The Harmonica Sandwich 5
Breathe Easy 5
Harmonica Tablature 6
One Man Band—Chording the Blues 7
Slip-Sliding Along 7
    When the Saints Go Marching In 8
    Harmonica Lament 8
    High Lonesome Whistle: Train Blues 9
    Chasing the Train 9
I Got Rhythm 9
Time Signatures 10
Ties 10
Blues Rhythm 10
Swing Eighths 11
    I Yam What I Yam 11
    Back Porch Blues 11

Chapter 2—Single Note Blues 12
Pucker Up! 12
Tongue Blocking 13

Chapter 3—Reading Music 14
The Staff 14
The Notes on the Staff 14
Ledger Lines 14
    Ready and Rarin' to Go! 16
    When the Saints Go Marching In #2 17
Hand Vibrato 17
    Hair of the Dog Blues 19

Chapter 4—Straight-Harp Blues 20
    When You're Dead, You're Done 21

Chapter 5—Cross Harp Blues, Bends and More 22
Get the Bends: Draw Bends 22
Sharps and Flats 23
Possible Draw Bends for the First Six Holes 24
More Draw-Bending Licks 26
The Shake 26
    Lonesome and Blue 27
    That Gets My Goat 27
Diaphragm Vibrato 28
The Blues Scale 29
    Scales for the Halibut 29
    OO-Wee! 30
Vocal Effects: Shouts, Moans, Wails and Cries 30
The Twelve-Bar Blues 31
Accompanying 32
    Bargain Bass-ment Blues 32
    Complementing Blues
            (or "Gosh You Look Swell") 33
The Blues Rumba 34
    You Rumba Me the Wrong Way 34
Blow Bends 35
Blow Me Down—Possible Blow Bends
            on Your C Harp 36
More Blow-Bend Licks 37
The Swoop 37
    Blue Lights, Blue City 38
A Sense of Wonder 39
    Boogie on Stevie! 39

Chapter 6—Minor Blues 40
    Twelve-Bar Minor Blues 40
Soloing in Minor 41
    One Room Lonesome Country Shack 42
    How Could A Woman Be So Mean? 43
    This Pain in My Heart 43

Afterwords—The Road Goes on Forever 44

Appendix 1—Troubleshooting 45
Appendix 2—Blues Keys for Each Harmonica Key 46
Appendix 3—All Available Notes on C Harmonica 47
Appendix 4—Essential Blues Harmonica Listening ... 47

About the Author

Rob "Fletch" Fletcher lives in a one-room country cabin in the foothills of the Shawangunk Mountains in New Paltz, New York. He teaches private music lessons and classes in environmental education. He has performed with Trey Anastasio of Phish and Ronnie Earl, among others, and is a teacher at the National Guitar Workshop. He holds a Bachelor of Music in Jazz Performance degree from the State University of New York at New Paltz. Fletch spends as much time as possible outdoors. He travels throughout the world whenever he can, and loves to find beautiful places and good people with whom to share his harmonica playing.

Track 1

A compact disc is available for this book. This disc can make learning with this book easier and more enjoyable. This symbol will appear next to every example that is on the CD. Use the CD to help insure that you are capturing the feel of the examples, interpreting the rhythms correctly, and so on. The track numbers below the symbols correspond directly to the example you want to hear. Track 1 will tell you how to use the CD. Have fun!

Introduction

Welcome to the wonderful world of blues harmonica! This book is written for YOU, the blues harmonica beginner. The harmonica, or "harp," which is its affectionate nickname, is an amazing instrument! It fits in your pocket and goes wherever you go. You can play it while walking around, whether in a forest or on a city street. Whenever you have a spare moment, pull it out, knock out the lint and the spare change and blow!

The harmonica is the only instrument on which both exhaling and inhaling are used to create different notes. It has a rich capacity for soulful expression because of its closeness to the human voice, both in sound and where it is physically held. It is a small, wind-powered instrument whose notes can be bent and shaped to express whatever feeling or longing is inside you. Plus, harmonicas are cheap! The humble harmonica can truly be called the people's instrument.

You will need a harmonica in "the key of C" for all the songs and licks in this book (and to play along with the optional CD). If you already have a harmonica, look to see what key it's in. The letter is stamped to the left or the right of the holes, or on the top of the harmonica (where the numbers I through 10 are printed). If it says "C," you're in luck! If it's in another key, you need to buy one in "C" but don't throw out the one you have. Later in the book you'll learn when to use harmonicas in other keys. Good harmonicas with which to begin learning are the Hohner Special 20, the Huang Silvertone and the Lee Oskars.

Your journey begins here. Savor each moment in the learning process. This is a great chance to have fun! Also, the songs and licks you'll be learning are ultimately just tools for you to shape and play in your own style as you progress and find your own unique "voice" on the harmonica.

Let's get started!

Dedication

This book is dedicated to Chris Burger for introducing me to the blues and to harmonicas; Jerry Mueller (my favorite sax player) for inspiring me to go further and deeper into this sweet life; Joseph Jastrab for guiding me through the wilderness; Ma and Pa Fletcher and the rest of the Fletcher clan for your love; Ronnie Earl for showing me the soul and the beauty of the blues; Kevin Doell for solid friendship; and Vanessa Hein for eight sweet years; "love is thicker than forget."

Acknowledgments

Thanks to Junior Wells, Little Walter and Howard Levy for playing the harmonica with fire and creativity, and Pat Bergeson for keeping my harmonica horizons open from the beginning. Also, thanks to Walter Hardy, Bruce Schnieder, Gwen Saylor, Chris White and Karen Schmieder. I carry your hearts with me.

Thanks to the Blue Rays (bassist Robert Burd, drummer Gary Schwartz and guitarist Chris Vitarello) for their playing on the CD.

Special thanks to Hohner, Inc. for their generous photographic contributions to this book.

Chapter 1

Holding the Harmonica—The Harmonica Sandwich

Place the harmonica in your left hand as if it were a sandwich, with the thumb on the bottom and the index finger on the top cover plate. The middle finger is nestled against the back. The numbers I through 10 are embossed on the top. Number I is to the left as you are playing, 10 is on the right and the sounds go from low (left) to high (right). The right hand thumb is next to the left thumb, both thumbnails are facing you and the palms are together. The rest of the fingers of the right hand curl over the left hand. Make sure your hands feel relaxed and comfortable.

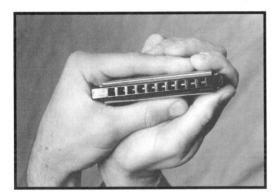
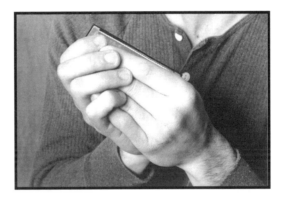

Breathe Easy

Put the harmonica in your mouth, being as careful as possible to hold it correctly. Breathe in and out anywhere on the instrument. As long as you're hearing some kind of sound, you're doing well. Keep breathing without taking the harmonica out of your mouth. If you can last a full minute without feeling strained from lack of air, you have discovered the secret of harmonica breathing.

Open your throat and allow the air to flow deep into your belly. The chest should be relaxed and seem to be only a passive observer watching as the air flows deeper into the stomach. The stomach expands outward to let air in and then pushes inward to send air up and out.

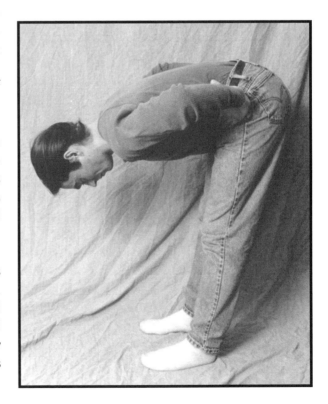

Here is an exercise that will help you learn what this action feels like. Bend over as if to touch your toes. Put your hands on your sides and with your head still down, breathe. You'll feel your stomach and sides fill up and then contract. Your chest feels completely bypassed. The secret to a good harmonica tone lies in breathing in that same way when standing up.

Harmonica Tablature

In order to communicate musically, we have to agree on a way of writing harmonica music. We'll start with a system of harmonica tablature that corresponds to the numbered holes on your harmonica.

You will see numbers with arrows below them. If the arrow is pointing up, blow out (exhale) on that hole. This is called a blow note. If the arrow is pointing down, draw the air in (inhale) on that hole. This is called a draw note.

Blow	**123**	Draw	**234**
Blow out on holes 123 at the same time.		Draw in on holes 234 at the same time.	

Beats are the basic way to measure time in music. When you tap your foot to a tune, you're tapping beats. Beats are the backbone of a song and are steady like your heartbeat, a clock or your feet when walking. The duration of a note—how long it lasts—is measured in beats. A note can last for one beat (a quarter note), two beats (a half note) or four beats (a whole note). A note can last less than a beat, too, as in eighth notes (half of a beat, two per beat). Here is a chart showing how these durations will be written in harmonica tablature:

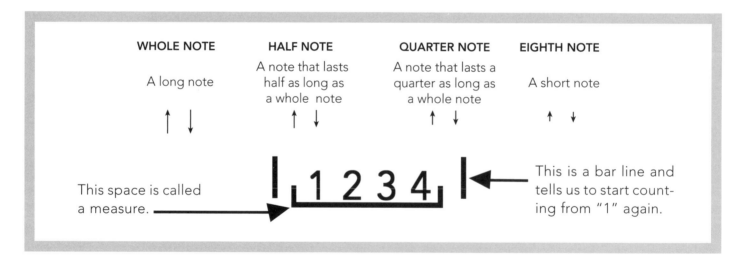

Play all the music in this book slowly at first and then increase the speed once you feel steady and comfortable. A great tool to help you with this is a metronome. A metronome clicks out a steady beat (quarter notes) for you to play along with and can be found in any music store. Most of the songs in this book have a metronome marking next to them. This is a recommended tempo (speed) for that song. If that tempo is too fast, start slower and then increase the speed. The tempo symbol shows a music note (a quarter note ♩) equaling a specific number of beats per minute. Here is what they look like:

$$♩ = 120$$

One Man Band—Chording the Blues

You are now ready for your first blues riff! It uses *chords*. A chord is any group of at least three notes played together. This one is located on the lowest three holes, and it is not necessary to move your harp to play the example. The beats that say "rest" over them mean exactly that: don't play any notes, just rest, get your breath back and prepare to play it again.

1
Track 2

$\bullet = 80$

123	123	123	123	123	Rest	Rest	Rest
↓	↓	↑	↑	↓			

count: 1   2   3   4 | 1   2   3   4

Let's jazz it up by adding something on the third beat in the second measure.

2
Track 3

$\bullet = 80$

123	123	123	123	123	Rest	234	Rest
↓	↓	↑	↑	↓		↓	

count: 1   2   3   4 | 1   2   3   4

Slip-Sliding Along

Let's practice moving around! Keep your mouth on the harp at all times while moving from hole to hole. Never break contact. Slide up and down on one exhale. Repeat it while breathing in. Keep your lips loose and relaxed. If they stick to the harmonica, lick them.

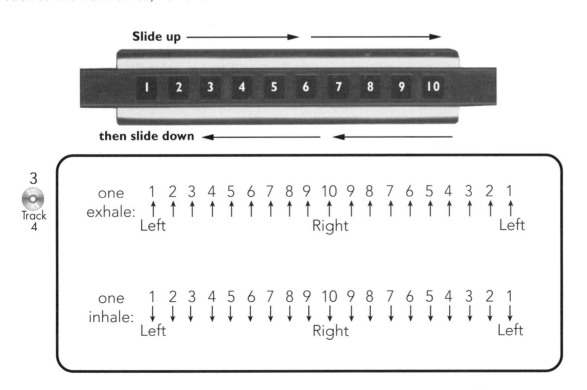

8

Here is a classic song to play. *When the Saints Go Marching In* is very well known and you will surely know the tune. Follow the general contour of the melody; it's not yet necessary to play the exact holes written. Just move it around in that general direction until it sounds right to your ears. If only two notes sound sometimes, that's fine, too. The notes in parentheses are optional—they are a background/accompaniment. It isn't part of the melody; it makes the song sound fuller. Add them when you feel comfortable with your breathing.

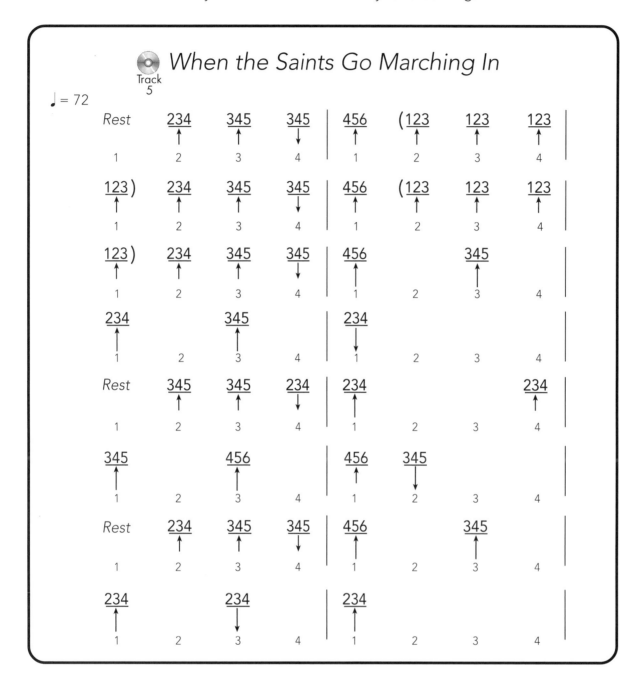

The next song is a "lament," which is a long, time-honored tradition in music. What does it sound like? Imagine missing the person you love most, or a deep, unfulfilled longing that burns inside you. The lament is a musical expression of that feeling. Check out jazz saxophonist John Coltrane's *Lonnie's Lament* for inspiration. Every musician worth his salt knows at least one good lament. Here's yours! Hole 4 can be added if it feels comfortable. Inhale as long as you can, then exhale as slowly as you are able. The double bar line with dots is called a *repeat sign*. Always repeat the music that precedes it at least once. In this case, repeat until the tears become too numerous. End on an inhale!

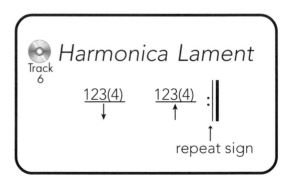

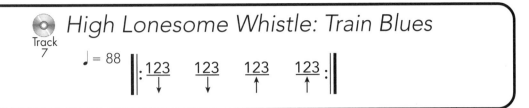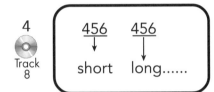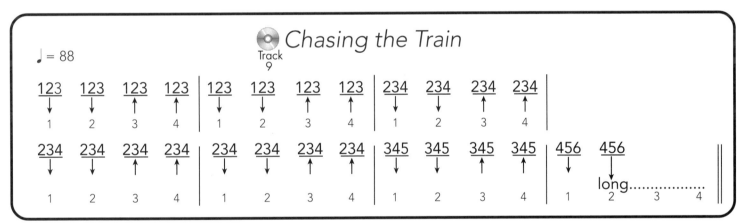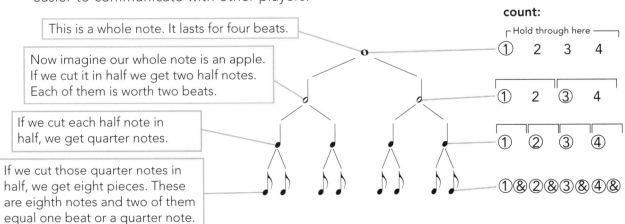

The harmonica has a deep capacity for expression. It has been used to imitate a human voice crying for help, a baby, an accordion and even a coffee percolator! But by far the most imitated sound is that of a train.

Play each chord equally and crisply. Start off slowly as the pistons and wheels start to move. Then increase the speed as you feel more comfortable and the train starts moving down the tracks.

Now add the whistle, one short then one long blast in the middle of the harmonica.

Start each note with a closed hand position and then move to an open position. As the long note ends, close it again.

Let's use the long blast in a song.

I Got Rhythm

It's time to learn the standard system for writing note durations. This will make it easier to communicate with other players.

This is a whole note. It lasts for four beats.

Now imagine our whole note is an apple. If we cut it in half we get two half notes. Each of them is worth two beats.

If we cut each half note in half, we get quarter notes.

If we cut those quarter notes in half, we get eight pieces. These are eighth notes and two of them equal one beat or a quarter note.

Time Signatures

All the songs in this book have four beats in each measure. This is shown with a *time signature*. The top number tells us that there are four beats in each measure and the bottom number tells us that the quarter note equals one beat.

$$\frac{4}{4}$$

Ties

A tie combines two notes of the same *pitch* (highness or lowness of sound) so that they sound as one long note. The second note isn't played separately. Rather, its value is added to that of the first.

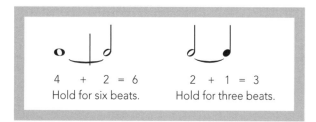

4 + 2 = 6
Hold for six beats.

2 + 1 = 3
Hold for three beats.

Blues Rhythm

Blues rhythm is unique. It's like playing a waltz in each quarter note. This is done by stuffing three notes into each beat. We call this an *eighth-note triplet*. Let's try a measure of triplets. Say "oom-pa-pa" aloud as you clap along. Then try saying "1-po-let, 2-po-let," etc.

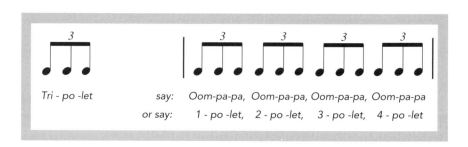

Tri - po -let

say: Oom-pa-pa, Oom-pa-pa, Oom-pa-pa, Oom-pa-pa
or say: 1 - po -let, 2 - po -let, 3 - po -let, 4 - po -let

Try it on the harmonica:

5

Track 10

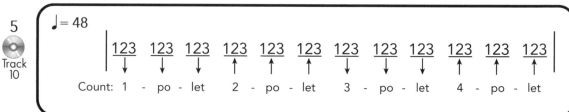

♩ = 48

123 123 123 123 123 123 123 123 123 123 123 123

Count: 1 - po - let   2 - po - let   3 - po - let   4 - po - let

Now let's tie the second triplet eighth note to the first. This creates a long—short, long—short rhythm. Try saying "Jell–y Bell–y."

say: jell - y, bell - y, jell - y, bell - y,

Try it on harmonica:

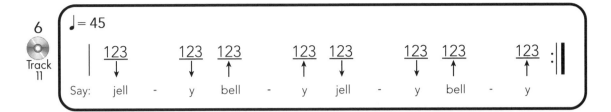

Swing Eighths

This is the rhythm found in almost all blues songs and is called a *swing eighths* or *shuffle* rhythm. Swing eighths are written like regular, even eighth notes... ♪♫
...but played with a swing feel. In this book, you will also find the word "swing" written at the beginning of songs with swing eighths.

Here's a great riff in the style of Muddy Waters' song *I'm a Man*. The most challenging part is the triplet on the fourth beat. If you have the CD that is available for this book, before playing along say "I Yam What I Yam" along with that part of the lick. Also, if you're having trouble breathing, don't play the notes that do not have words underneath. They are optional. Swing the eighth notes on the third beat.

Imagine a lazy summer evening for this one.

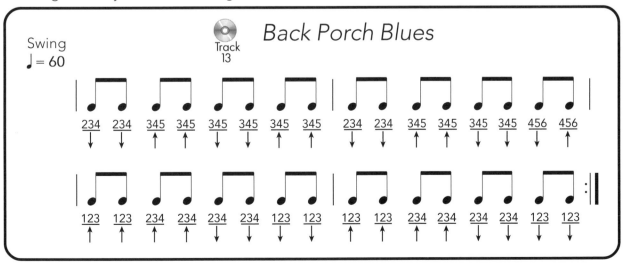

Chapter 2

Single Note Blues

Pucker Up!

Welcome to the world of the single note! This is the basis for all blues solos and melodies so let's dive right in! The easiest way to get a single note is with a technique called *puckering*. Say "shhh" as if you were trying to quiet a small child. Notice the shape of your lips as you do this. Now place the harmonica between your lips and blow. Start on the 1-hole, the lowest sound on your harp.

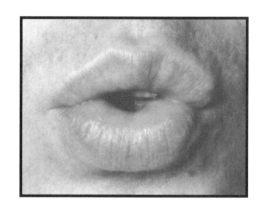

Here are some hints to help you:

First, the lips themselves should be loose and relaxed—don't purse them. It's the ring of muscles behind them that do the work, not the actual lips. Suck your cheeks in so that they look hollowed. Think of blowing a kiss to someone or whistling.

Tilt the harmonica up a little and put two-thirds of your upper lip onto the top cover (directly against your hand). Put one-third of your bottom lip on the bottom cover. Looking into a mirror is helpful for this. Don't be shy, the harp is your friend!

If you still hear more than one note, or the single note sounds weak and airy, you probably don't have your lips far enough out on the harmonica cover. Puckering is not like sipping a cup of tea! Think more of gulping down a mug of coffee. Your lips form a harmonica sandwich with plenty of harp between them.

Once you've successfully gotten a clear sound with the hole 1 blow, try the hole 1 draw. Then move over to hole 2 and then up and down the entire harmonica, concentrating on getting a nice clear tone on each hole.

Tongue Blocking

The other method of getting a single note is with a technique known as *tongue blocking*. As with the chord playing in Chapter 1, your mouth should be wide open, letting three or four holes sound at the same time. Now place your tongue down on the holes of the harp on one side of your mouth, either left or right. This blocks air from entering most of the holes and allows only one to sound. Placing the tongue on the left side of the mouth usually works best. This makes a high note sound.

Start with any hole you like. Blow out first then draw in. Once you can do this, place your tongue on the right side of the mouth. This makes a low note sound. Now move your tongue back and forth, alternating between high notes and low notes *without moving your mouth on the harmonica*. You're doing great!

Blocking low notes to sound a high note:

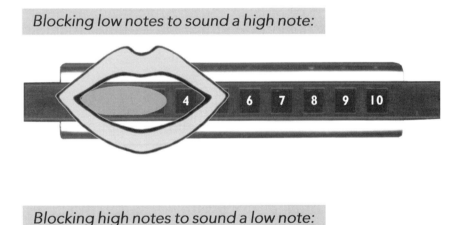

Blocking high notes to sound a low note:

Tongue blocking is not an essential technique to master in the very beginning, but is an important tool for your blues soloing toolbox. It can also be used for many fun and interesting effects that can't be done using the pucker method—so it's worth it to practice!

Chapter 3

The Staff

Standard music notation is written on a system of five lines and four spaces called a *staff*. It is read from left to right. At the beginning of every staff is a symbol called a *clef*. Even though there are other kinds of clefs, the *treble clef* 𝄞 is at the beginning of all harmonica music. This clef is sometimes called the *G clef* because its tail encircles the "G" line.

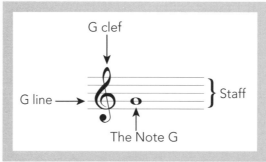

The Notes on the Staff

Every line and space on the staff has a note name from the musical alphabet. The musical alphabet starts on A and goes up to G. After G, it starts again with A. The treble staff lines are E, G, B, D and F as in "Every Good Boy Does Fine." Another fun sentence might be "Elephants are Great But Dance Funny." Come up with your own acronym. The spaces spell FACE. Remember, "the FACE is in the space."

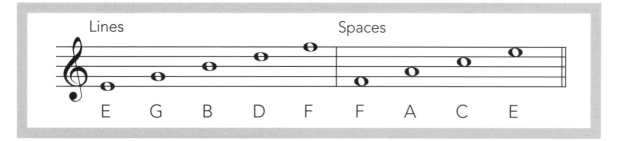

Ledger Lines

Sooner or later you will want to play notes higher or lower than the nine lines and spaces. Don't panic. We have a system called *ledger lines*. They are short lines that are written above or below the staff to show higher or lower notes than the staff will accommodate.

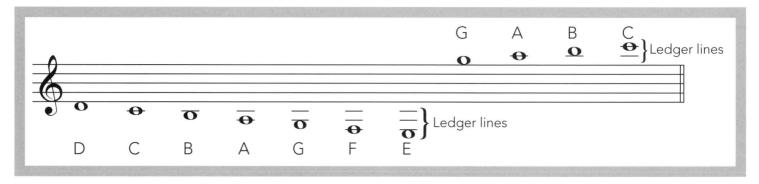

Even some experienced musicians have difficulty reading an extreme number of ledger lines. For this reason, we use the *8va* symbol, called *all'ottava*. This means to play the same note one *octave* higher than written. An *octave* is the closest distance between any two notes with the same name. For instance, you can play a low C or a high C. They are an *octave* apart and they are the same note, but one is higher than the other. The example below shows how this symbol can be used to simplify reading the high E.

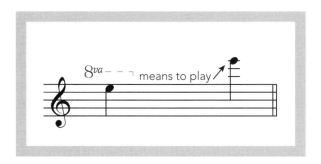

Below are all the notes you can play on your harmonica with the techniques you have learned so far. If you play them in alphabetical order, starting on the note C, they comprise the *C Major scale*: C, D, E, F, G, A, B, C. Notice that in the lowest octave (C to C) the F and A are missing, and in the highest octave, the B is missing. In the middle octave, though, all the notes are present. Practice playing the scale ascending and descending.

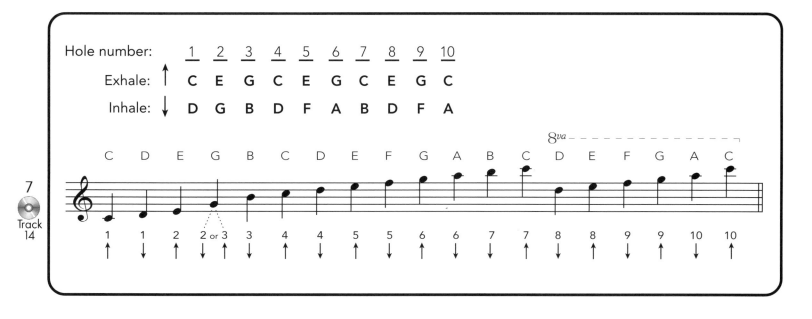

16

Here are your first single note blues licks! They are a great warm-up for the next song, so make sure you've got 'em down before moving on.

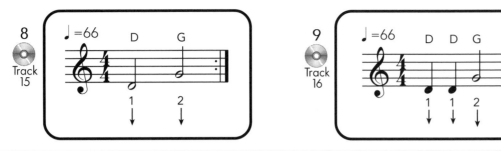

If you don't want to play, you can *rest* (and breathe!). Here are how two important rest values are shown in music notation:

Half rest (two beats)   Quarter rest (one beat)

Have fun learning your first full blues tune. This song has a repeat sign, so is played twice. After playing it the second time, play the measure that appears after the repeat sign.

Ready and Rarin' to Go!

After you repeat, play this measure to end the song.

Congratulations on learning your first single note blues song! Now take the licks in this song and rearrange them any way you like to make your own version of the song. If you have the CD, play your version along with *Ready and Rarin' to Go*. Be creative! Next, play whatever you like on the harp. Most of the notes will work with this song. This is called *improvising* and is the foundation of blues music. Experiment in this way with all the licks and songs in this book and they will become your own.

TIP
While improvising, focus on drawing in on holes 1 through 5, the bottom half of the harp. These will sound best.

Here is the classic tune you learned on page 8, but now in a single-note version. This will get you reading quarter notes, half notes, quarter rests and half rests on the staff.

Hand Vibrato

Vibrato means a gentle wavering of the tone. All of the great harmonica players use vibrato to add depth and character to their sound. To get vibrato on your harmonica, open and close your cupped hands. Keep the heels of your palms together and open and close your right hand. This will alternately mute and open the sound, causing the vibrato effect. Start it SLOWLY. Once you start getting a change in sound, try gradually increasing and then decreasing the vibrato tempo.

Open

Closed

If you're having difficulty, take the right hand totally off the harmonica and sound a note. Slowly bring the hand back and then take it off again. This shows how a vibrato sounds. Also, leaving your hand off is useful for a more wide-open sound in the style of Sonny Boy Williamson II.

It's time to practice your eighth notes (see page 9 for a review)! This lick will prepare you for *Hair of the Dog Blues* on page 19. Remember to swing the eighths (see page 11).

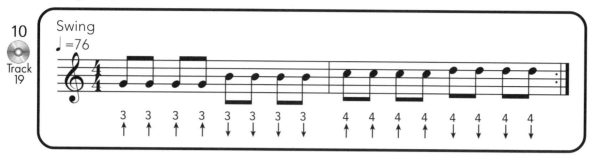

The following two licks will get you moving around on the harp more, preparing you for the leaps in *Hair of the Dog Blues*.

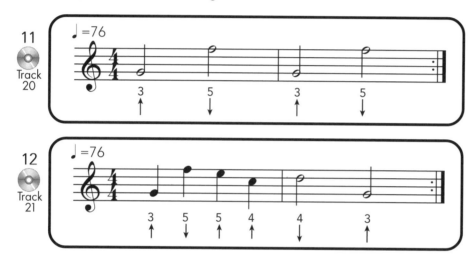

Sonny Terry

was a master of acoustic country blues playing. He was born in rural Greensboro, Georgia and learned harmonica from his father, a field laborer. In 1940, he teamed up with guitarist Brownie McGhee. He created a warm, exuberant harp sound utilizing driving rhythms and vocal shouts.

Sonny Boy Williamson II

was a blues storyteller. He began his recording career in Mississippi in the early 1950s but, like most post-war blues artists, he ended up in Chicago recording for Chess Records in 1955. His songs contained striking imagery and every note in his solos was well placed and came from deep inside. He wandered everywhere and played with everyone from Robert Johnson to The Yardbirds. His outrageous, flamboyant lifestyle and hard living are reflected in the intensity of his music.

PHOTO CREDIT - COURTESY OF HOHNER, INC.

Here's a new rest for you to learn:

Eighth Rest
½ beat

Look at the last measure of the second line (the eighth measure) of *Hair of the Dog Blues*. There is an eighth note rest ( ) on the first part of the third beat, followed by playing on the "&." This kind of *off-beat* rhythm is common. Try counting aloud and clapping this rhythm before playing the song.

Hair of the Dog Blues

Chapter 4

Straight harp is a very simple concept. In straight-harp, you play in the key of your harmonica. So, with your C harp you will be playing a blues in C!

The focus in straight-harp is on a new area of the harmonica, the top half. This is where most of the great straight-harp virtuosos play. Two great players to listen to for inspiration are Jimmy Reed and Stevie Wonder.

Let's start out with some easy licks. Examples 13 and 14 are in the style of Duke Ellington's famous song, *C-Jam Blues*. Notice the use of the *8va* sign to make reading the high notes a bit easier (see page 15).

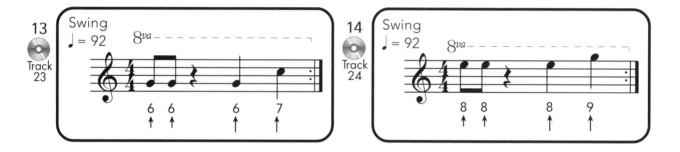

Here are some that will get you moving around the harp a little more. Also, notice that tied notes (see page 10) are very important aspects of the rhythm.

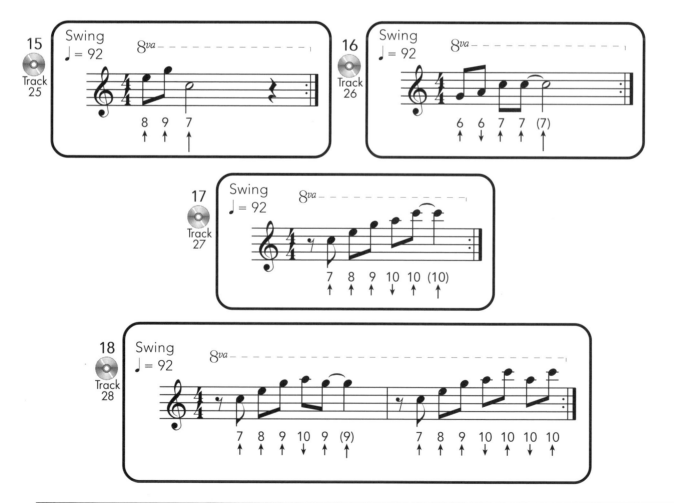

A dot after a note increases its duration by half its value. For instance, a half note is two beats. Half of that is one beat, so a dotted half note is 3 beats (2 + 1 = 3). Any kind of note can be dotted.

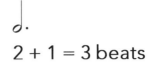

2 + 1 = 3 beats

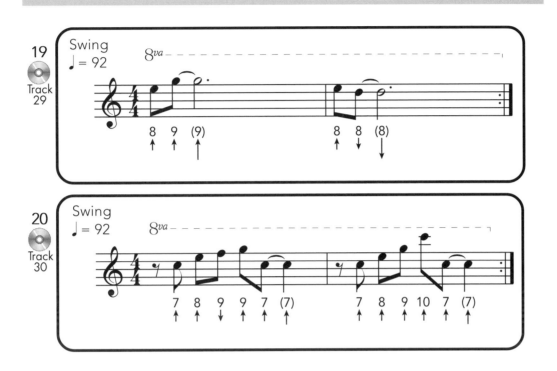

Enjoy playing this straight-harp tune.

Chapter 5

Cross-Harp Blues, Bends and More

Most blues harmonica is played in cross-harp. This means that your harmonica is in one musical key (C) while the actual blues song is in another (G). We do that because those "bluesy" notes are only available to us when we use a different key harmonica than that of the song. Also, when we *bend* notes (hang in there, just wait till we get to the bottom of this page), they sound best in cross-harp.

A simple rule to figure out what key works best for your harp is to count up five letters in the musical alphabet including its key.

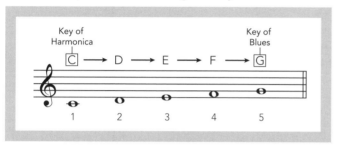

If you know the key of the blues song and are wondering which harp to use, count up four letters in the musical alphabet from the key of the song.

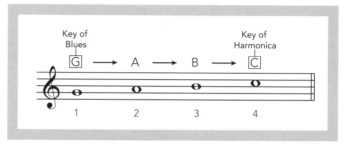

Overall, this works well. However, there are a few exceptions. For a complete listing of all the cross-harp relationships, see the table on page 46.

Get the Bends: Draw Bends

Bending is what gives the harmonica its wailing, moaning quality. It also provides a number of new notes we can't get any other way. Draw bends lower the notes on the bottom six holes.

Half Steps and Whole Steps
Now that you're going to be bending notes, it's important to understand the distances between them. The two most important distances are the *half step* and the *whole step*. The whole step is a bigger distance than the half-step. The distance from E (hole 5 blow) to F (hole 5 draw) is a half step. Look on a piano keyboard. You'll see white and black keys. The distance between any two adjacent keys is a half step. The distance from C (hole 1 blow) and D (hole 1 draw) is a whole step. On a piano keyboard, the distance from one white key to another (where there is a black note between them) is a whole step.

Here's how we notate a half step draw bend:

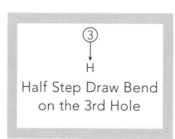

H = Half Step
W = Whole Step

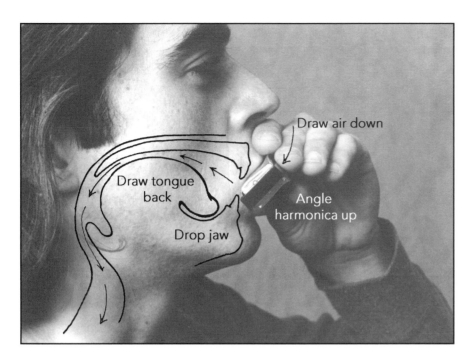

When we bend, we are redirecting the air-flow as it enters the mouth and throat. Imagine drawing the air downwards, curving and swallowing it.

Your tongue, which is normally in the front of your mouth against your teeth, is drawn to the back of the mouth. Think of a piston as you keep the tip of the tongue against the bottom of your mouth and draw it back. It is difficult to position your tongue this way if you are using tongue blocking. For this reason, try using the pucker method (see page 12). It will be much easier.

At first, it is also helpful to drop your jaw down, as if you were hanging your mouth open. Also, angle the harmonica even higher in the air as you continue to imagine those notes being swallowed and bent down.

Start on any of the bottom four holes. You may find this difficult, but don't despair! Now is a good time to practice patience. Have faith because the bend WILL come. Just devote a few minutes each day to practice this and suddenly a bend will appear. Once you've gotten the idea, it will stay with you forever. Just like riding a bicycle—you won't forget. Once you have a bend, hold it down as long as you can. If it flits back up, bring it down again. This is a good exercise to help develop control.

Sharps and Flats

Flat

The flat means to lower the note one half step. This is your first *accidental*. An accidental is a sign used to raise, lower or return a note to its original pitch. Its effect lasts through the remainder of the same measure. For instance, a draw on hole 1 is D. If this D note is preceded by a flat sign ♭, it means to draw bend that note down a half step.

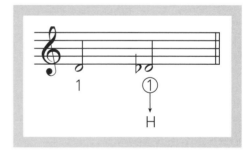

Sharp

The sharp raises the note one half step. For example, the D♭ above can also be called C♯.

Natural

The natural returns a note that has been raised or lowered to its original position.

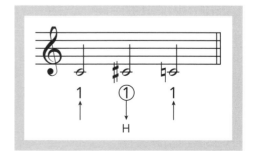

Let's try two easy half step draw bend licks to get the ball rolling. Be patient with the material in this chapter. No one expects you to learn to bend overnight. It may take weeks to get the hang of it, so hang in there!

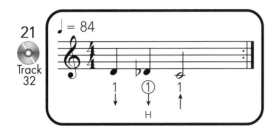

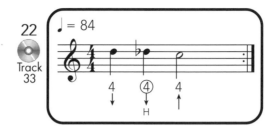

Possible Draw Bends for the First Six Holes

This section is provided as a resource for you to come back to again and again. It is not realistic to think that you will sit down one afternoon and learn all of these bends! Learn them one at a time. Get comfortable with them—they will travel with you forever. So, make bends part of your daily practice and continue through the book. As bends come up in the songs, refer back here and learn them.

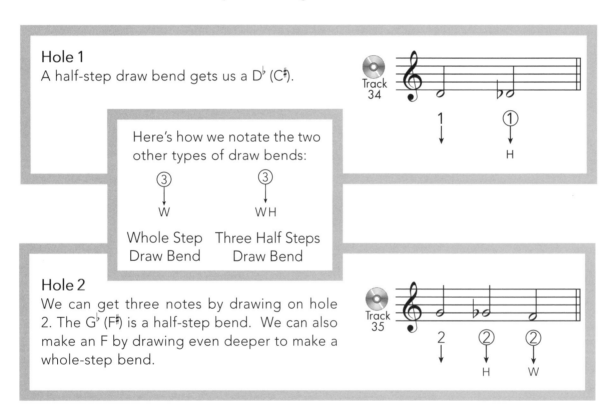

Hole 1
A half-step draw bend gets us a D♭ (C♯).

Here's how we notate the two other types of draw bends:

Whole Step Draw Bend   Three Half Steps Draw Bend

Hole 2
We can get three notes by drawing on hole 2. The G♭ (F♯) is a half-step bend. We can also make an F by drawing even deeper to make a whole-step bend.

Hole 3
This is the motherlode! We can draw bend three new notes. To get the A♭ (G♯), you have to execute a whole-plus-a-half step draw bend. Draw down deep! With increased opportunity comes increased difficulty. It's hard to get these accurately, so be patient! You can master them with practice.

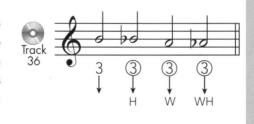

Hole 4
Same as the I hole but an octave higher.

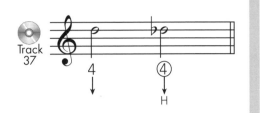

Hole 5
You can't really get a bent note on hole 5. It's only a slight lowering of sound but it sounds great! Think of this bend as being less than a half step. Call it a *quarter-tone bend* (hence the "¼" marking in the music).

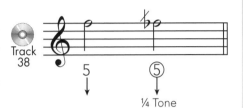

𝄳 = A quarter tone. A note which is halfway between an F and an F♭.

Hole 6
A half-step draw bend gets us an A♭(G♯).

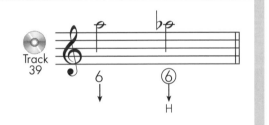

All notes available on bottom 6 holes.
Here is a summary of the notes available on the bottom 6 holes. This includes blow notes, draw notes and draw bend notes.

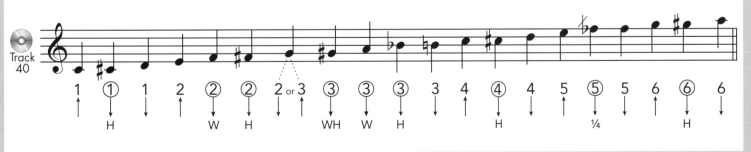

More Draw-Bending Licks!

Practice all of these licks until they are smooth and quick.

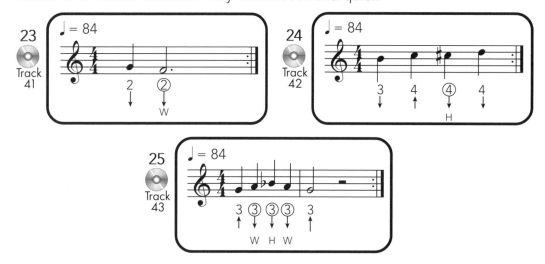

The Shake

The shake is the harmonica's version of a *tremolo*, which is a rapid alternation between two notes. The two notes blend into a unique sound.

The technique is a gentle combination of subtle head and hand movements. Start on one note. Slowly move over to the higher note, then back. Repeat this, gradually gaining speed. The eighth notes should be even, not swing eighths.

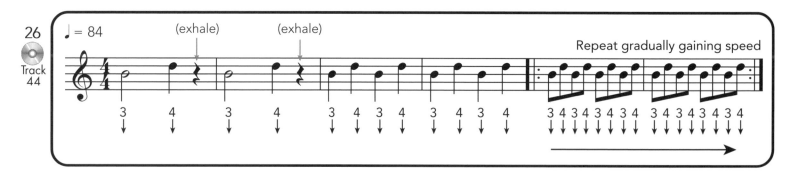

Each note should be equally loud and clear. People tend to overdo it and blaze out a swathe of notes from holes 1 to 10 while wildly shaking their heads. Go for accuracy first (just two holes) and work on the speed of the shake later. Here is an exercise to help you develop the technique. Practice all three of the following shakes every day. Eventually, you'll be a master of the shake. Shake notation shows both of the notes in the shake. For instance, the B-D shake in Example 19 lasts for just two beats, even though it looks like two half-notes.

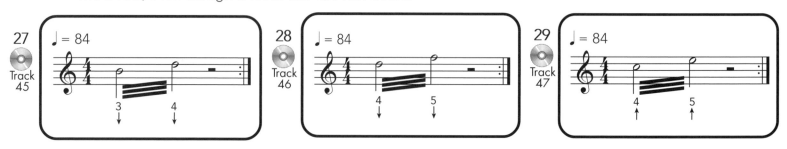

The shake sounds great, is fairly simple to do and fits well into any blues solo. It's also a great thing to do while you're thinking of other melodic ideas!

Here is a song in the style of Little Walter. The chords to the song are shown above the staff so that a friend can play along. Notice the triplet in the third measure (see page 10).

This song is in the style of Sonny Boy Williamson II. Pay special attention to the rhythm in the third measure. The measure begins with an eighth note rest and the G (hole 3) comes in off the beat, on the "&" of "1." Then there is a triplet on beat four (4-po-let). It would be helpful to practice counting aloud and clapping the rhythm before trying to play the measure.

Diaphragm Vibrato

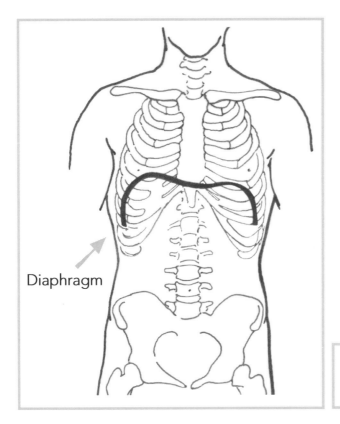

Diaphragm

This type of vibrato is created by pulsing your breath. Say "uh uh" as if someone had just asked if they could play your new harmonica. Now keep saying it, as if they really don't understand what "NO" means. Now do it silently. Focus on your diaphragm or stomach pushing up pulses of air. Imagine that you are breathing pulses of air on a mirror to wipe a smudge off. Now try it blowing out on any hole on your harp.

The same principle applies for the draw notes but in reverse. With each pulse of air you take in, picture your stomach expanding as if it were hooked up to a bicycle pump.

The *diaphragm* is the partition of muscles and tendons between the chest cavity and abdominal cavity.

James Cotton

"Mr. Superharp," started out in Muddy Waters' band in the 1950s. A dynamo of joyful blues playing, he was the original inspiration for the Blues Brothers. He often plays at reckless tempos, has been known to do somersaults on stage and cave in the cover plates of his harps just from the force of his playing!

PHOTO CREDIT - ROBERT BARCLAY / COURTESY OF HOHNER, INC.

The Blues Scale

The blues scale is a helpful guide for choosing what notes to use in your solos.
Here it is in the key of G:

Here are the locations for all the notes in the G Blues scale on your C harp:

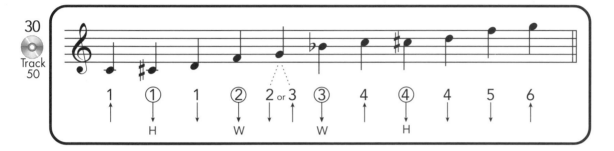

Here's a cool blues tune that uses the G Blues scale. The last four bars include
some wide leaps in the melody, so practice slowly.

Scales for the Halibut

This exercise will prepare you for the fifth and sixth measures of the next song, *OO-Wee!* Use a very slow diaphragm vibrato technique on the hole 2 draw bend. Hold the hole 2 draw bend and take little breaths deep into your belly. Do it slowly and you'll hear a separate note sound each time you inhale.

This tune is in the style of Junior Wells.

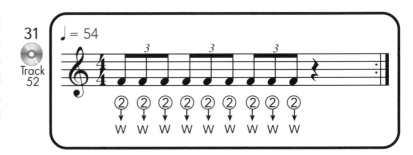

OO-Wee!

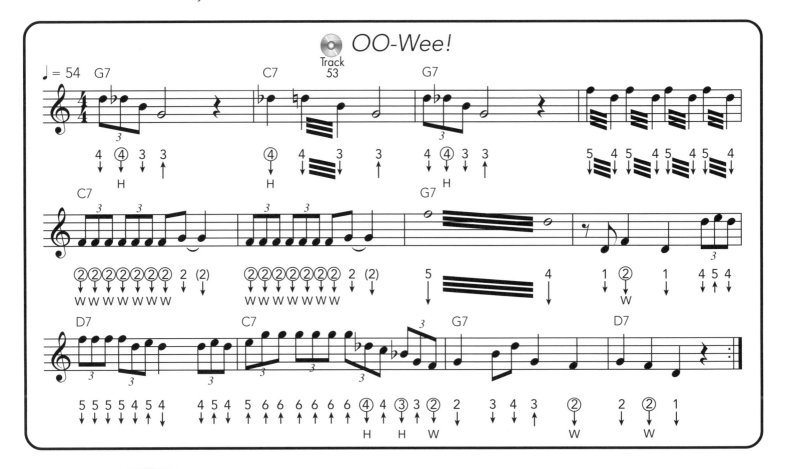

Vocal Effects: Shouts, Moans, Wails and Cries

An easy and fun way to spice up your playing is to add vocal effects. Shout, scream or speak anything you want into the harmonica. The effect is often eerie and can add a great deal to a solo. Another approach is to whoop or shout away from the harp and then go back to your solo. Sonny Terry and Junior Wells are masters of these concepts. Also check out guitarist Clarence "Gatemouth" Brown's rare forays into harp playing.

Another trick is to make the harmonica speak, using the bent notes and hand positioning. Separate each vowel of what you want to "say" by using the diaphragm technique. Hand vibrato technique is useful as well. Close your hands at the beginning of each vowel, and then open. The diaphragm and hand vibrato techniques combined give the effect of speech. Try alternating between a bent and un-bent note for an even better result. Here is an example:

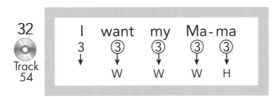

The Twelve-Bar Blues

It is important to know what the form of the blues is.

Most blues songs have a twelve measure (also called *bar*) form that repeats. There are three chords within these twelve bars. We call them I, IV and V. Roman numerals are commonly used to describe chords. For those of you who are skipping Latin class to learn harmonica instead, here's a review of Roman numerals:

Roman Numerals				
I	**II**	**III**	**IV**	**V**
1	2	3	4	5

The numberings for these chords come from their positions in the key. As you know, you are playing a C harp. In other words, if we are playing a G blues, which is what we do on a C harp, the I chord will be G. If you are soloing, your guitar player will be strumming a G chord when I is called for. If you count up four in the musical alphabet from and including G, you get C (G, A, B, C). Your guitar player will be strumming a C chord when IV is called for. Count up one more letter in the musical alphabet to find V and you'll find D. Your guitar player will be strumming a D chord when V is called for.

Each of these three chords has its own unique sound and different notes will sound "right" over each. To the right is a typical twelve-bar blues chord pattern. Memorize this pattern.

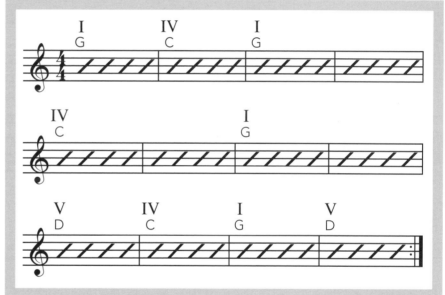

As you know, you can play chords on the harmonica, too. Learn these chords, since you'll need them in the next section.

I The **I** (G) chord is found on the 1 - 5 draw notes.   123↓ 234↓ 345↓

IV The **IV** (C) chord is found on the 1 - 10 blow notes, although the lower notes sound better.   123↑ 234↑ 345↑

V There is no **V** (D) chord available, so either play the I draw or I and 2 draw together.   1↓ 12↓

Accompanying

Accompanying, or *comping*, is adding chords or background to support another musician. This art is especially valuable for those times when it's just you and another harmonica player. One of you accompanies while the other one solos. Sensitivity is important; whatever you play must complement the soloist. In this section we will explore chordal accompaniment, bass lines and single note riffs.

A great way to accompany is to play a bass line. Imagine you're the bass player for this one.

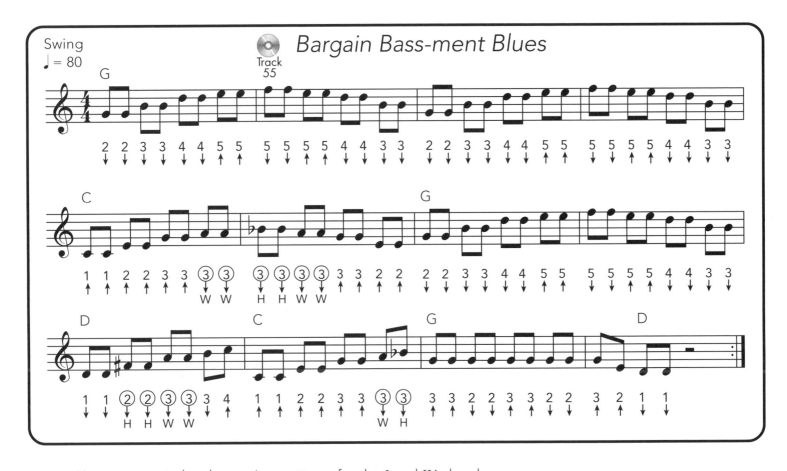

Here are great chord-comping patterns for the I and IV chords.

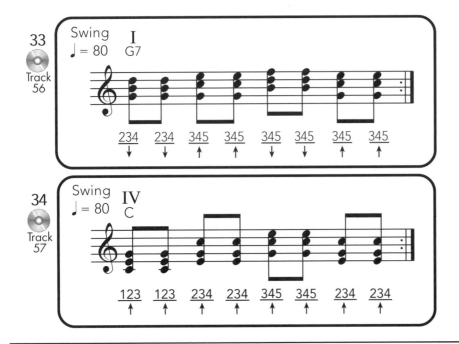

1st and 2nd Endings

This song uses 1st and 2nd endings. When you come to the repeat sign (see page 8) go back to the beginning. Then play up to the 1st ending, skip it, and continue with the 2nd ending to the end.

Little Walter

Little Walter is thought by many to be the most influential harmonica player ever. He had his own unique style. Whether playing with Muddy Waters in (starting in 1948), or on his own, his playing displayed almost a jazz sound over swinging blues backgrounds. His gorgeous phrasing is reminiscent of a jazz saxophonist and his amplifled sound revolutionized blues harmonica.

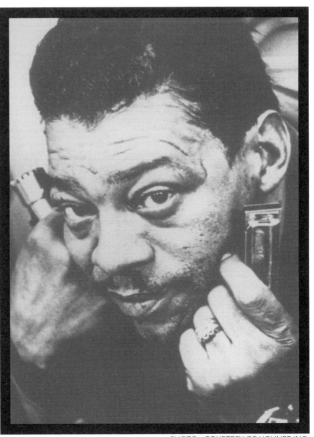

Big Walter "Shaky" Horton

was an undersung hero of the blues harp. He was a consummate sideman and can be heard playing backup harp on countless vital blues records of the 1950s and '60s, as well as on his own recordings . He had a spacious sense of time and his note choices were faultless. Above all, his deep and gorgeous tone, a tone every harp player dreams of having, was unparalleled. He wasn't into harmonica acrobatics. Rather, he conveyed his message through his amazing sound and feeling.

The Dotted Quarter Note

See the top of page 21 to review dotted notes.

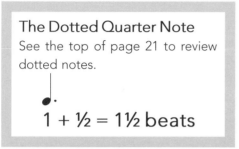

1 + ½ = 1½ beats

PHOTO - COURTESY OF HOHNER INC.

The Blues Rumba

The blues rumba is a great accompaniment pattern for straight harp. What a wonderful sound! It is characterized by this rhythm:

1 & 2 & 3 & 4 &

Enjoy this rumba tune.

Some great blues rumbas to check out are:

Early in the Morning	Louis Jordan
I Don't Play	Little Walter
La Cucaracha	Walter Horton
She's Into Something	Muddy Waters
Too Many Cooks	Robert Cray
Who's Been Talking?	Robert Cray
Woke Up This Morning	B. B. King

You Rumba Me the Wrong Way

Blow Bends

Blow bends are notes that can be bent while blowing out. This is a difficult technique and you will probably need to revisit this section a few times before you are comfortable with blow bending. Blow bends can be done on holes 8, 9 and 10. The lower the pitch of the note, the easier it is to bend, so we'll start with hole 8. Following this reasoning, it's a good idea to get a few lower-pitched harmonicas in different keys, such as G, A♭ and A. This will make practicing easier and then you can switch up to the C harp. In fact, most blow-bend players only play in these lower keys. Jimmy Reed's two biggest hits, *Bright Lights, Big City* and *Honest I Do* are played on an A harp, while Stevie Wonder favors A♭ for *Boogie On Reggae Woman.* However, all the licks and songs in this chapter are on the C harp.

The technique involved in blow bends is the same as draw bends, but in reverse.

Here are some tips for making a blow bend:

- The air is blown forcefully out and down.
- The tongue is placed against your lower front teeth throughout.
- Your air stream becomes narrow, and it may help to bring your teeth closer together (not touching), as if you were a fish breathing underwater.
- If you can whistle, whistle a note and then lower the note. Notice what your tongue does when you lower the note. It does the same thing to get a blow bend.
- A good exercise to focus on directing your air stream is to place the heel of the palm of your hand against your chin. Hold out your hand horizontally and blow out, directing the air down into your palm while holding your head straight.

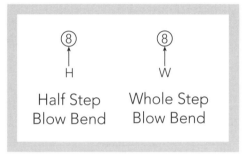

Half Step Blow Bend Whole Step Blow Bend

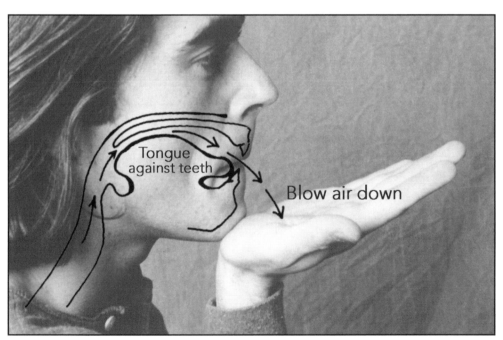

Once you feel the air in your palm, try it on hole 8 of your harmonica. Visualize the air entering and bending down the little reed that is inside the harmonica.

If you don't get it right away, keep working at it—don't give up! As with the draw bends, if you keep trying, at some point it will just magically happen and you'll wonder what seemed so hard five minutes ago.

The first time you get it, the note may sound a little ragged and flutter back and forth from bent to unbent. A simple exercise for this is to hold the bend down as long as you can. Don't release it. If it flutters back up, take a breath and bend it back down. Do this until the bend feels easy to control or until the neighborhood dogs start howling. Once you've got the hole 8 bend, move up to 9 and then 10 (10 is a hard one, so be patient).

Try these basic blow-bend licks on for size.

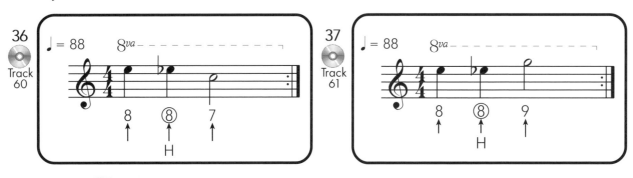

Blow Me Down—Possible Blow Bends on Your C Harp

As with the draw bends, be patient. Learn these one at a time.

Hole 7
As in the hole 5 draw, you can't get a full note bent, just a lowering of the note (about a quarter-tone) but it sounds great!

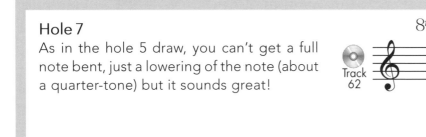

Hole 8
We can blow-bend an E♭.

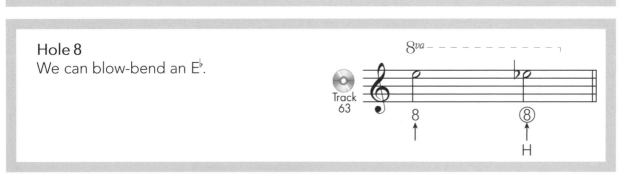

Hole 9
We can blow-bend a G♭.

Hole 10
These are hard to play accurately but worth the practice.

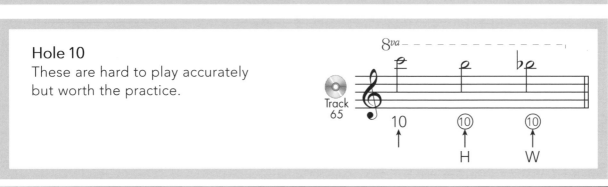

More Blow-Bend Licks!

Have fun!

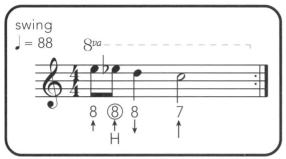

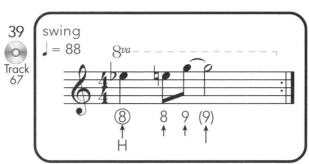

The Swoop

The *swoop* is a great blues harp technique. Like so much about the blues, it is highly expressive and hard to define. To execute a swoop, start with a bent note and slide up to an unbent note on the same hole. Make it as smooth and fluid as possible, making one continuous sound. It is notated like this:

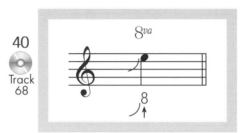

TIP

The swoop technique is very effective when combined with a closed-to-open right-hand movement, making a "wah" sound.

PHOTO - COURTESY OF HOHNER INC.

Jimmy Reed

had a sweet and easily accessible harmonica sound that has been widely appreciated and imitated. Playing harp in a mouth rack as he played guitar, he had hit after hit on the R&B and Pop charts in the 1960s. This was a rare feat by a pure bluesman which has perhaps only been surpassed by B. B. King. His sweet, yearning vocals and relaxed, laid-back blues have inspired many rock bands and solo acoustic artists.

Blue Lights, Blue City is in the style of Jimmy Reed.

TECHNIQUES TO ADD TO YOUR PLAYING

The Tah

The tah adds a percussive sound to a note. Say "tah." Now make the "t" sound only, first while exhaling, then while inhaling. The inhale "t" feels strange at first, but it will soon become second nature. Play any exhale note on the harp and make the "t" sound at the same time. Once you hear an audible difference, repeat it with an inhale note. To some extent, almost every major harp player uses this sound. It helps to separate notes and adds a driving, funky sound that sounds great!

The Trill

The trill is an interesting effect that, when used judiciously, is a great way to spice up a solo. It is the same technique as rolling the "r's" in the Spanish language. Form an "r" and roll or flutter your tongue. Wind instrumentalists, such as flutists, call this a *flutter-tongue*. Imagine you're a kid making motorboat or car engine noises. Now do that on a single-note exhale (this effect is only practical on the exhale). Check out Big Walter Horton, De Ford Bailey and Stevie Wonder to hear some great trills. Don't be alarmed if you can't do this. It's one of those things like the ability to roll your tongue into a tube...it's genetic.

A Sense of Wonder

Stevie Wonder is a great source for blow-bend ideas. His playing is extraordinarily rhythmic and his jagged, joyfully vocal harp style is infectious. Warmth and whimsy flow out of every line he plays, inviting a smile from all who listen.

Practice the licks on the right to prepare for *Boogie on Stevie*. They are from the more technically difficult parts of the song. Also, the Stevie licks and song do not use the swing rhythm that all our other songs have used. In this book, this will always be notated as "Straight Eighths" at the beginning of the tune. Just give each eighth note an even, equal amount of time. If you like, try using the tah you've just learned.

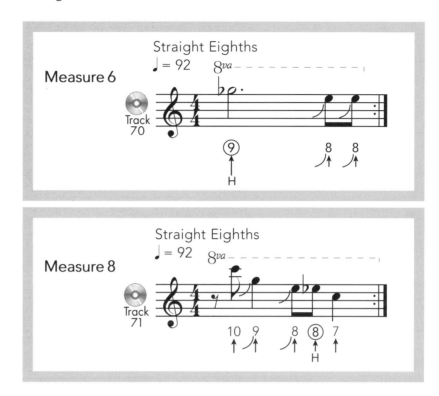

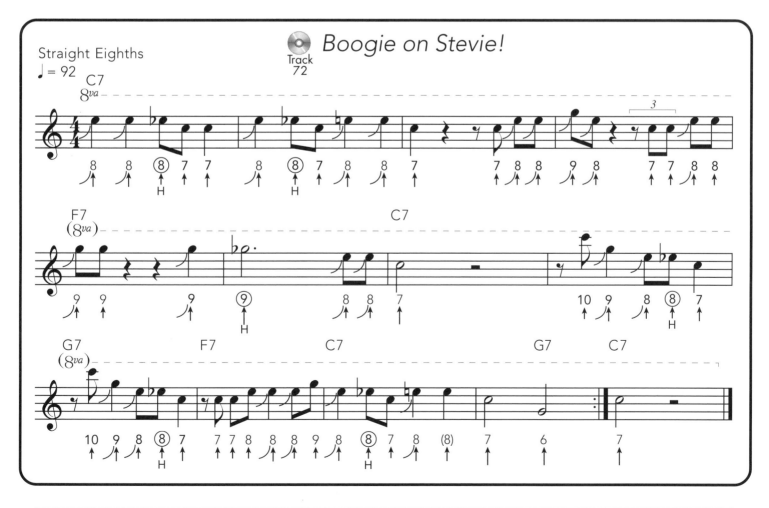

Chapter 6

Minor Blues

Up until now, all of our blues songs (in cross-harp and straight-harp) have been in a major key (G and C). We're going to explore minor keys. A minor key blues has a unique sound. It is sadder and more intimate-sounding than the major key blues. Deep emotion and feelings such as despair, yearning, longing and quiet sadness can be expressed more easily.

Some popular minor key blues songs are:

As the Years Go Passing By .... Albert King
I Feel Bad, Bad, Bad .... Carey Bell
I'll Play the Blues For You .... Albert King
In the Wee Hours .... Junior Wells
Must I Holler? .... Carey Bell
Pleading the Blues .... Junior Wells
Ships on the Ocean .... Junior Wells
Slow Slow .... Junior Wells
The Thrill is Gone .... B. B. King

You can get an idea of the sound from the song titles alone.

To figure out what key the minor blues would be in for your harmonica, go one letter above the key of your harp. For example, your C harp is good for playing the D Minor blues. If you know the key of the song and want to know what harp to use, go down one letter. For example, if the key of the song is D Minor, use your C harp.

This works well, overall. However, there are exceptions. Check out the handy chart on page 46 for all the possibilities. What this means is that now we can play in three different keys (C Major, G Major and D Minor) with one little old harmonica. Life is good!

As before, in Chapter 5, it is good to know what the blues form is, and here it is in minor. The small "min" stands for minor and the lower case Roman numerals (i = 1, ii = 2, iii = 3, iv = 4 and v = 5) also signify minor chords.

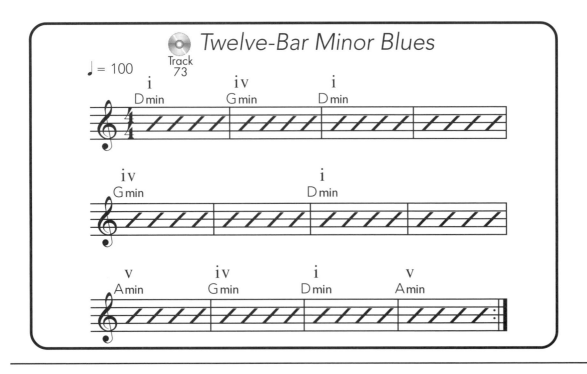

Soloing in Minor

Soloing in a minor key is a special treat. Due to the emotionally bare sound of the music itself, almost anything you lay on top of it sounds good. Here are some helpful guides:

Use the Middle Octave
You may have noticed that the bulk of your cross harp playing is in the lowest octave (holes 1 to 4). In straight-harp, most of the licks are in the highest octave (holes 7 to 10). In minor blues, the middle octave is most used (holes 4 to 7). Any note in this octave will sound great!

Remember the Four Minor-Blues Home-Base Notes
There are four notes that are safe to play anywhere on the harp. Let's call these the *four minor blues home-base notes*. They are:

Here's where they can be found on the entire harmonica:

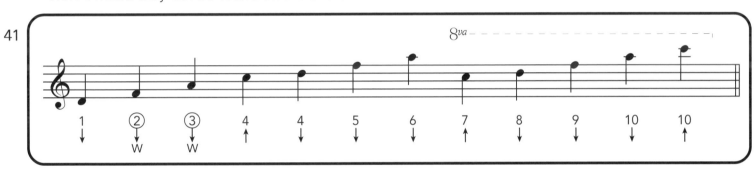

Below are some minor blues licks to get you started. Master each one and you'll be ready for the tune on page 42.

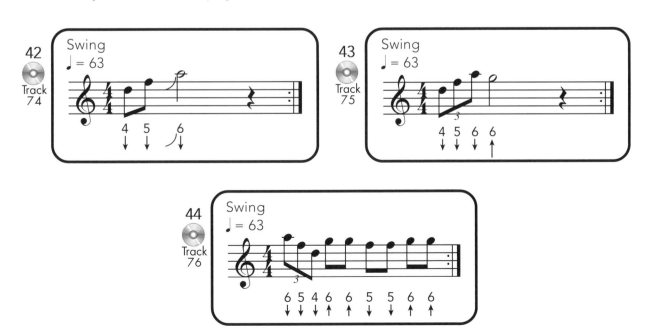

The quick leap in the ninth measure and the precise hole 3 bends in the tenth measure will need some special attention. Practice these measures slowly before attempting the whole song. Have fun!

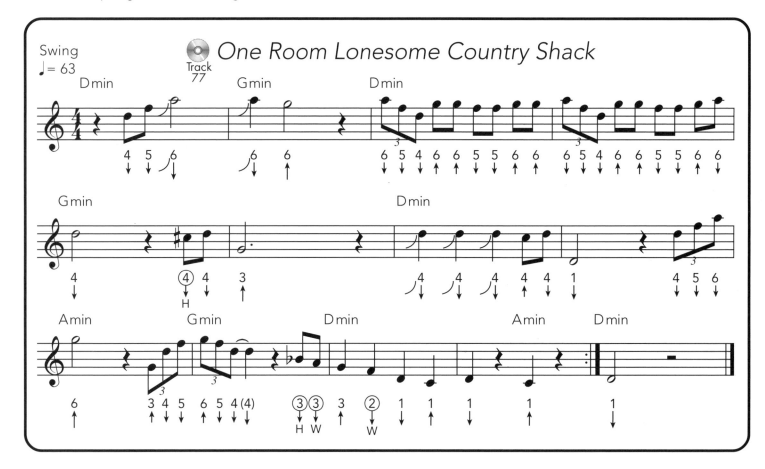

ANOTHER TECHNIQUE TO ADD TO YOUR PLAYING

Meet the "Fast-Moving Shake." This effect is in the "easy-to-play-and-sounds-hard" department, which is a very good department indeed! This is an all-inhale, every-hole lick. Start out with a high shake on holes 9 and 10 and move down, hole-by-hole, until you reach hole 1. It's a fairly quick move, all in one fluid motion. Don't worry about accuracy, play it with joyous abandon! Listen to Carey Bell for inspiration.

The example below approximates the sound of this technque. Since some of the notes are very high and a bit tricky to read, there's a small, alternate staff (an *ossia* staff) showing the the highest notes with an 8va for easier reading.

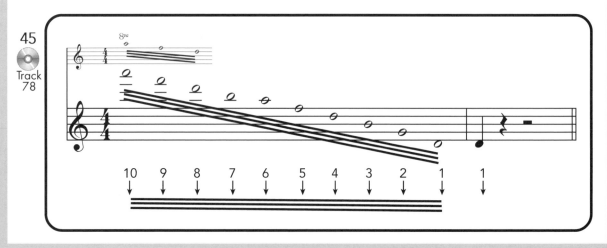

This song is in the style of Junior Wells. Give some extra practice to the precise bends in the fifth measure and the triplet lick in the sixth measure.

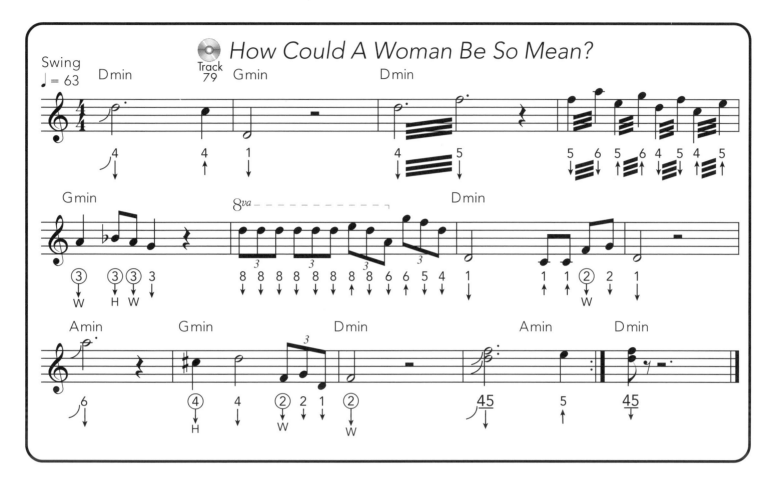

Here is a great pattern for accompanying a minor blues.

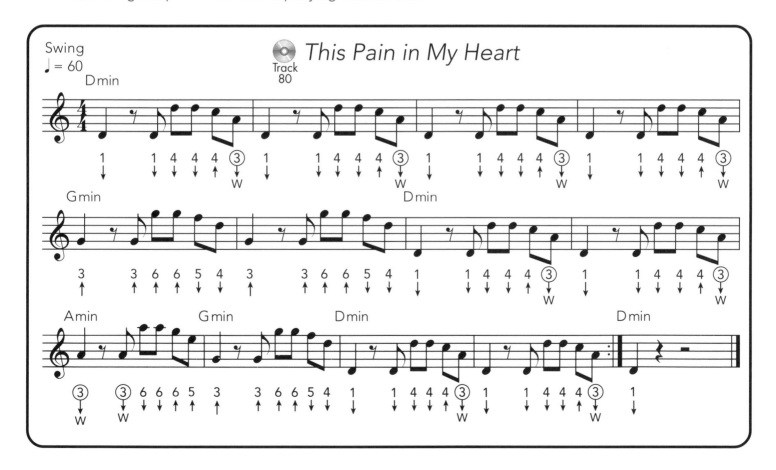

Afterwords

The Road Goes on Forever

This is just the beginning! There are so many exciting possibilities for you and your harmonica. Check-out the artists listed on page 47 and try to play what they play. Try playing jazz, rock, country, polkas, Indian ragas, classical music, sea chanteys or whatever you desire. Also, try playing along with any song, no matter what the key, with your C harmonica. Two other keys you should definitely explore are E Minor and A Minor. There are harmonicas available in different tunings—try them out. Also, try a chromatic harmonica. Play with a friend. Play with several! Bear in mind that there were all-harmonica groups and orchestras in the 1920s and '30s that used harmonicas in numerous keys and sizes. It could happen again!

Music is one of the sweetest gifts, a friend in times of darkness and joy. Teach a loved one how to play, take it outside into the sunlight and fresh air. The road goes on forever! Learning music is not a journey to get anywhere particular, just to be fully alive right where we are. If you were to reach a final goal, it would be all over and, as the song says, "when you're dead, you're done." Playing harp is about expression, getting what is inside you out into the open air and having it resonate with others. We all share this love of music. Play well!

PHOTO - COURTESY OF HOHNER INC.

Junior Wells,
"the Hoodoo Man,"

was the master of funky, soulful harp playing. Like many of the greats, he started out with Muddy Waters. Also one of the finest blues singers ever, he had a long and fruitful solo career, both on his own and in collaboration with Buddy Guy. His work with Buddy in the 1960s and '70s taps into the very heart of the blues and is some of the finest music ever recorded. "The undisputed godfather of the blues," he had an amazing sense of phrasing and his harp solos employed wails, vocal yelps, clicks, pops and other sounds. He created his own unique sound out of the legacy of the early players and will continue to inspire future generations of harp players.

Appendix 1

Problem	Try This...
airy sound	Put more of the harmonica in your mouth (remember, two-thirds on top and one-third on bottom).
can't bend	PATIENCE, PATIENCE, PATIENCE! They WILL come. Draw your tongue back, draw the air down and in, drop your jaw, tilt the harp up.
can't get just one note	Get more of the harp in your mouth and/or shift harp a little to left or right; sometimes we are in between holes without realizing it.
can't find the right hole	Take the harp out of your mouth, put fingers on either side of the hole and play the note. Remember the sound and put your tongue against it so you can find it when your fingers are off. Repeat this. Every time you do it, you'll improve.
can't make wide leaps	Practice them very, very slowly at first. Always keep the harp in your mouth and lick your lips for clear sailing!
getting headaches or sore mouth	This means you're tense somewhere. Try to sense where in the song the tension starts. Watch yourself in a mirror while you play. Breathe into the tense spot, releasing the tension that's there and give gentle attention to it every time the tension returns. Stop if you get dizzy.
hard to move mouth across harp	Lick your lips and relax.
one note sounds very, very strange, or won't sound at all	Knock harmonica against your hand, blow into back. If problem persists, use a small screwdriver to remove screws and take off cover plates. See if there's any lint, hair or foul demons in the reed (a thin peice of metal that vibrates to create the sound). GENTLY lift up reed from inside of the harp with the screwdriver and blow the offending particle out.
reeds are getting clogged with spit	Knock harmonica against your hand, blow strongly into back from a few inches away, swallow spit in your mouth before you start playing.
short of air, not enough breath	Remember, every draw note means you're receiving new air. Some people draw in, but don't let the air that comes in with the note into their lungs. Relax and let this air in!
tongue blocking—sounding more than one note	Move tongue a little to the right if you're getting a note from the right side of your mouth. Move tongue to the left if you're getting a note from the left side.
tongue blocking—no note	Move tongue a little to left or right.

Appendix 2

Blues Keys for Each Harmonica Key

Harmonica Major Key	Harmonica Minor Key	Cross-Harp Key	Straight-Harp Key
C	D Minor	G	C
C#	E♭ Minor	G# (A♭)	C# (D♭)
D	E Minor	A	D
E♭	F Minor	B♭ (A#)	E♭ (D#)
E	F# Minor	B	E
F	G Minor	C	F
F#	G# Minor	C# (D♭)	F# (G♭)
G	A Minor	D	G
A♭	B♭ Minor	E♭ (D#)	A♭ (G#)
A	B Minor	E	A
B♭	C Minor	F	B♭ (A#)
B	C# Minor	F# (G♭)	B

How to Find the Key of a Song on a CD and What Harmonica to Use

Your best education is listening to the masters and trying to play what they play. The challenge is to figure out what key a song is in and in what position (cross, straight, minor) it is played. There are two ways of finding the key of a song. They both involve listening to the bass player. Using either a C harmonica, guitar, piano or bass, play the lowest-sounding bass note at the beginning of the song. This is also the note most often played throughout a song. It helps to sing it and hold the pitch either aloud while you find it on guitar or piano or in your mind as you search for it on your harp. This note is the root of the I chord and is the key of the song.

Once you know the key, try the harmonica that fits in cross-harp. The bulk of blues harp is in cross-harp. If it doesn't fit because the song is high, bright and cheery, try straight-harp. If it needs to sound sadder, try the minor position.

The other approach is a bit more random. Try all the harps you have (hopefully, in all twelve keys). Either try to play some of the licks with each one or find the first bass note. If you're playing in cross-harp, the bass note of the song should be the same as the hole 2 draw or hole 3 blow.

This is an interesting education and opens up new possibilities because you may stumble on a harmonica key that isn't the one used but sounds good anyway! This process is time-consuming, but it opens up a whole new world. Good luck and savor the process of discovery!

Appendix 3

All Available Notes on C Harmonica

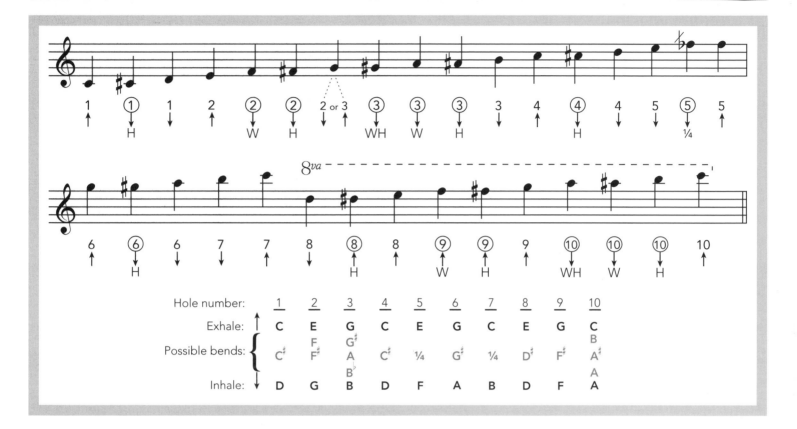

Hole number:	1	2	3	4	5	6	7	8	9	10
Exhale: ↑	C	E	G	C	E	G	C	E	G	C
Possible bends: {		F	G♯							B
	C♯	F♯	A	C♯	¼	G♯	¼	D♯	F♯	A♯
			B♭							A
Inhale: ↓	D	G	B	D	F	A	B	D	F	A

Appendix 4

Essential Blues Harmonica Listening

Title	Record Label
Big Walter Horton — With Carey Bell	Alligator
Blues Masters Vol. 4, Harmonica Classics (Compilation)	Rhino
Brownie McGhee and Sonny Terry Sing	Folkways
Essential Blues Harmonica (Compilation)	House of Blues
James Cotton — Best of the Verve Years	Verve
Jimmy Reed — Live at Carnegie Hall/Best of Jimmy Reed	Mobile Fidelity
(not a live album and not recorded at Carnegie Hall)	
Junior Wells — Hoodoo Man Blues	Delmark
Junior Wells — It's My Life, Baby	Delmark
Little Walter — His Best	Chess / MCA
Muddy Waters — His Best	Chess / MCA
(any Muddy Waters CD will have great harmonica playing on it)	
Sonny Boy Williamson II — His Best	Chess / MCA

The list could go on for a few more pages but these will get you started. There's a stunning amount of blues harmonica CDs available, so indulge! Also, several of these people are still touring and recording. James Cotton, Carey Bell and Snookie Pryor, among others, continue to play amazing blues. Latter day innovators to check out are: Gary Primich, Paul de Lay, Kim Wilson, Charlie Musslewhite, Billy Branch, Annie Raines and Rod Piazza, among others. See these people live. The blues is a living art that flourishes with human contact. Have fun!